LEAD

TO
SUCCEED
AND YOU WON'T
MANAGE
TO
FAIL

WRITTEN BY   COREY W. GRANT

Published by the International Leadership Corporation, A Delaware Corporation

Website:
http://www.leadershipcorporation.com
Facebook:
http://www.facebook.com/leadershipcorp
Twitter:
http://www.twitter.com/leadershipcorp

Lead to Succeed and You Won't Manage to Fail

LinkedIn:

http://www.linkedin.com/in/leadershipcorp

ISBN 978-0-9838559-0-3

This book was set in the font Times New Roman, 12 point on an Apple MacBook Pro by Corey Grant of the International Leadership Corporation.

10 9 8 7 6 5 4 3 2 1

Table of Contents

Biography

Corey Grant is a multi-faceted leader, business owner and graduate of both Southern University and Alabama A&M University, two of the premier historically black colleges and universities (HBCU) in the country. As a member of the United States Marine Corps, Corey honed his skills for leadership where he was taught the principles of adapting, adjusting and overcoming obstacles to achieve his mission and goals.

Corey has used his drive, determination and leadership style to progressively advance his career from an entry level staffer to leader of over $300 hundred million dollars in federal programs and services.

Forward

When deciding to write my first book it wasn't hard for me to decide a topic to write on. I've always heard successful people say find something you like to do and you will never work another day in your life. Simply put if you like something and you do it naturally, then the amount of effort is minimal and you won't worry or stress the same way people do when they have to constantly put an effort forward to achieve what may seem like a monumental task.

For me leadership is like breathing, I will do it until the day I die, whether consciously or sub-consciously it comes natural.

Leadership doesn't mean you can reach or teach everyone to adapt to your style, leadership simply means that there is some condition where you can excel, take charge, and get something accomplished in an environment where other people believe in you and your abilities enough to follow you there. Wherever there is.

When you can lead others to achieve their own success you will have succeeded many times over. A true leader helps others get to where they want to be.

Acknowledgements

First and foremost I want to thank God for giving me the life that I have and the wherewithal to write this book. My heavenly father has never let me down.

I want to thank my wife, Chantel, who supports my efforts, my career, and keeps me on my toes. The matriarch of the family, she has provided me with a beautiful family of three wonderful children, who provide me with endless challenges and amazements each and everyday. The glue that holds everything together with amazing style and grace, thank you, thank you, and thank you again from the bottom of my heart.

To my brother and sister, what else can I say but thank you for always believing in me no matter how crazy the idea seemed. In forty plus years we have never had an argument. That may not seem possible or mean much to others but it means the world to me.

To my friends, you know who you are, thanks for always being there when I needed you. You have helped me in more ways than you can ever know over the years.

To my mother and father. I think of you each and everyday for what you have both instilled in and done for me. I miss you dearly and I hope that I've made you proud. Rest in Peace and I will see you someday on the other side.

Peace and Blessings to All

Become a Management Legend

"YOU DON'T BECOME WHAT YOU WANT, YOU BECOME WHAT YOU BELIEVE." - OPRAH WINFREY

So you finally moved up and got promoted into management? That's what you've always wanted right? That's what you've been working toward your entire career. You were the career minded type with a plan to get where you are today, you have watched the chairs move, seen some people retire, watched others get promoted, maybe a few people even quit, got fired or were laid off. Nonetheless, you've made it to that vaulted plateau called management. Now what?

Now when you were devising your career plan and trying to figuring out which chairs would become vacant in your lifetime, which chairs you had to sit in to have the needed credibility for the next job, you assumed that the individuals sitting in those chairs had it made in the shade. They more than likely had an office

13

with a door and not a cubicle and if they were lucky, a window with a view to boot.

Fast forward to today!!! You are sitting in that office that you once coveted from afar and all the skeletons have fallen out of the closet. Along with those bones are the problems that you vaguely remember hearing stories about such as the grumpy employee that never completed a task on time or the rumored office tryst that no one could ever prove was really happening. Well now that you are here to save the day, all those bones are spread across the floor because surely you can fix what the last guy couldn't. Right?

In the world of wildland firefighting there are many different dangers that one can face. There are many factors that one must consider before blindly attacking the flames that will threaten the lives of brave firefighters, homeowners and property that lie in the path of destruction. The same can be said with managing people. Normally, you aren't so lucky that your first management job is one where someone says to you, "we are starting a new division and we want you to pick all the right people to make it run smoothly." If this happens to you please be sure to go to church on Sunday and standup to testify to the rest of the congregation about how God is good and has blessed you far beyond your wildest dreams.

So what do you do now that you've finally landed the job of your dreams? Now that you have walked into the belly of the beast and there is no turning back. In firefighting there are things you can check off on a list to make sure you have thoroughly prepared for, before implementing your plan of attack. In management you can sometimes get blindsided by a staffer or colleague before you ever make it to your office.

OK here is what you have hopefully done to prepare yourself for the flames that are waiting to burn you if you haven't prepared for them.

• Consult with the hiring official that gave you the chance to manage the organization that they are counting on you to save and find out what they really expect you to accomplish and in what timeframe

• Consult with the previous manager of the group if they are available to find out who are your go to players and who are your problem children.

16

- Determine what your goals and priorities will be for how you want to do business.

- Established what management style you want to use (and stick to it). It should be compatible with your personality.

- Determine what you would like your legacy to be (someday). This will help you determine what style will be most effective to get you there.

CHAPTER NOTES

Are You Cut Out for Leadership?

YOU CAN'T BUILD A REPUTATION ON WHAT YOU'RE GOING TO DO. -
HENRY FORD

Answer each of the following questions with an honest "yes" or "no."

- Do you believe that people are basically good and want to do the right things, even if they sometimes don't know what those things are or don't know how to do them?

- Do people naturally "come to you" and seek you out about things—interests, problems, joys, or just passing the time?

- Do you get along with most everyone? Oh, sure, there are a few difficult ones, but in general, can you co-exist peacefully with nearly everyone?

- Do you have passion or a strong enthusiasm for the organization and its mission?

- Are you approachable and available to those around you?

- Are you able and willing to communicate frequently and make communication a top priority in your leadership role?

- Do you possess a healthy measure of humility?

- Are you able to make firm decisions and take actions while, at the same time, taking into account the needs and suggestions of others?

Now depending on how you answered the preceding questions you should be able to gauge if being in a leadership position is right for you. Let's assess the results.

Did you answer NO and any question?

If the answer is YES then you might want to reassess your readiness for a leadership role.

Leadership and management are much more than telling other people what to do on a daily basis. Many people who are not in a leadership or supervisory position believe that their bosses simply wake up and come to work to tell them what to do while they sit back and do nothing. Now that's not to say that in some organizations that situation does not exist, but I would also dare to say that in that organization the supervisor is also probably not leading the staff very much either.

This is why I suggest you determine early on "what you want your legacy to be?" If you want to someday have a legacy as a leader then do you think that simply coming into the office and

22

telling people how many widgets they need to complete today will make you a management legend to be talked about around the water cooler 15 years after you have moved on? Not likely.

Management legends are people who have done great things for many people. The manager that was helpful, that chipped in when the workload was too much for the team to handle, that got rid of the bad apple or non-producers that everyone knew about but no one before them cared to deal with.

Becoming a management legend is going to require some work on your part, work that is more than issuing work orders for the day. How many times have you heard someone on your team or in your department say, "It's not my fault"? What about this one? "That's not my job." And I'll bet you've heard," 'They' didn't get me what I needed," and "Why does management keep doing these silly things?" Comments like these are everywhere in most of our organizations. Perhaps you have even said something like this yourself.

After all, YOU aren't responsible for everything that goes on in your organization…or are you?

One thing that sets managers apart is their ability to provide exceptional customer service. Customer service in the sense that they are not necessarily the person on the front line speaking to the customer that comes in with a problem, but they are the person that empowers the staff to be able to settle issues that affect the customer. Great customer service is also a manager's ability to see a problem that the rules say must be followed a certain way and instead they find a solution for the customer that is both legal and meets the customers needs.

There is no greater service one can give than that of himself. Ask yourself "how can I make a difference?" and you can.

CHAPTER NOTES

Leadership vs. Expertise

EXPERIENCE IS SOMETHING YOU GET A FEW SECONDS AFTER YOU NEEDED IT. - UNKNOWN

Leadership is not built on knowing more about "the WORK" than anyone else. No matter what your type of work is whether selling shoes, serving food, operating a computer, teaching grade school, playing a sport, or anything else you can think of, being the best at the work or task does not make you a leader. Being good at the work makes you an expert.

An expert is not the same as a leader and the sooner you realize that, the faster you will become a great leader. An expert is a go-to person concerning the job tasks. An expert CAN also be a leader but often is NOT.

People who are experts in the work to be done are often promoted to leadership positions because of their expertise. Expertise is an important quality, but it requires a completely different set of skills than leadership.

A good leader is often not an expert in the work and does not need to be. Leaders lead those who are experts in the work to be performed by providing clear direction and motivation. Leadership is about getting people motivated to achieve a distinct set of goals.

Leadership is about helping people achieve things that they didn't think they were capable of achieving. In addition, your own individual success in life is also largely dependent on the level of leadership skills you acquire. Anything you do in life, from your career to your personal relationships are positively impacted by improving your leadership skills.

If you have very few of these skills, you will always be limited in what you can accomplish. But you can learn, and you can do better.

CHAPTER NOTES

Leadership Styles

" A LEADER IS BEST WHEN PEOPLE BARELY KNOW HE EXISTS. WHEN HIS WORK IS DONE, HIS AIM FULFILLED, THEY WILL SAY: WE DID IT OURSELVES." — LAO TZU

There are many different leadership styles to choose from but the most important thing to do is to choose the right one for you, your personality and your situation.

From Mahatma Gandhi to Rudolph Giuliani, from Martin Luther King to President Barack Obama, there are as many different leadership styles as there are leaders. Fortunately, business people and psychologists have developed useful and simple ways to describe the main styles of leadership, and these can be used to help aspiring leaders understand which styles may work best for their circumstances.

Whether you are a team leader, a team captain playing sports, or you lead a major company, which approach is best for you depends entirely on YOU? Consciously, or subconsciously, you'll probably use some of the leadership styles discussed in this book. The key is understanding the different styles and letting them help you to develop your own, personal leadership style – and help you become a more effective leader.

With this in mind, there are many different styles that have shaped our current understanding of leadership, and if used appropriately they each have their respectful place in management. For the sake of this discussion we will look at some of the most common types of leadership.

Over the years researchers have developed a number of leadership theories. These can be categorized into four main types:

1. **Trait Theories** – What type of person makes a good leader?

Trait theories assume that leaders share a number of common personality traits and characteristics, and that leadership emerges from having these traits. Early trait theories promoted the idea that leadership is an innate, instinctive quality that you either have or don't have. Thankfully, we've moved on from this approach, and we're learning more about what we can do as individuals to develop leadership qualities within ourselves as well as others.

Trait theory does help us to identify some personal qualities that are helpful when leading others and, together, these emerge as a generalized leadership style. Examples include empathy, assertiveness, good decision-making, and likability. That being said, none of these traits, nor any combination of them, will

35

guarantee your success as a leader. You need more than that.

2. **Behavioral Theories** – What does a good leader do?
Behavioral theories focus on how leaders behave. Do they dictate what needs to be done and expect cooperation? Or do they involve the team in decisions to encourage acceptance and support?

In the 1930s, Kurt Lewin argued that there are three types of leaders:

Autocratic leaders are people who make decisions without consulting their teams.

Democratic leaders are leaders that allow the team to provide input before making a decision.

Laissez-Faire leaders don't interfere; they simply allow the team to make many of the decisions.

Each of these leadership styles will be discussed later in this chapter.

The **Blake-Mouton Managerial Grid** helps you decide how best to lead, depending on your concern for people versus your concern for production. The model describes five different leadership styles: impoverished, country club, team leader, produce or perish, or middle of the road. The descriptions of these will help you understand your own leadership habits and adapt them to meet your team's needs.

Figure 1: The Blake Mouton Grid

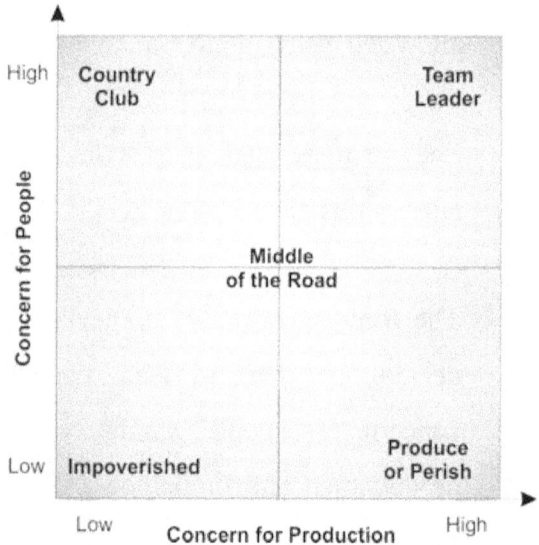

John Adair's Action-Centered Leadership model is another framework that's consistent with behavioral theories of leadership. Using this model, the "best" leadership style is determined by balancing task, team, and individual responsibilities. Leaders who spend time managing each of these elements will likely be more successful than those who focus mostly on only one element.

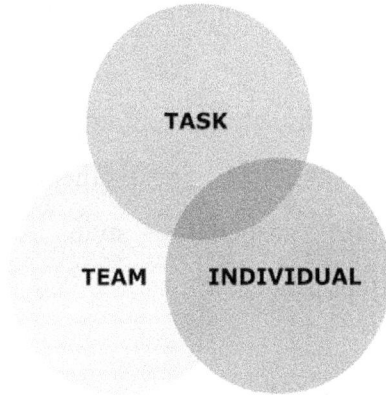

TASK

TEAM   INDIVIDUAL

The evidence clearly shows that how a leader behaves has a definite impact on their effectiveness. Researchers have realized, though, that many of these leadership behaviors are appropriate at different times. So, the best leaders are those who can use many different behavioral styles and use the right style for each situation.

3. **Contingency Theories** – How does the situation influence good leadership?

The realization that there isn't one correct type of leader has led to theories that the best leadership style is contingent on, or depends on, the situation. These theories try to predict which leadership style is best in which circumstance.

Should a leader be more people oriented or task oriented? When a decision is needed fast, which style is preferred? When the leader needs the full support of the team, is there a better way to lead? All these are examples of questions that contingency leadership theories try to answer.

4. **Power and Influence Theories** – What is the source of the leader's power?

These theories of leadership are based on the different ways in which leaders use power and influence to get things done. The most known of these theories is the French and Raven's, Five Forms of Power. The Five Forms of Power model looks at how leaders use their position to exert power or use their personal attributes to be powerful.

French and Raven identified three types of positional power: legitimate, reward, and coercive – and two sources of personal power: expert and referent (your personal appeal and charm). The model suggests that using personal power is the better alternative and, because Expert Power (the power that comes with being a real expert in the job) is the most legitimate of these, you should actively work on building it. Similarly, leading by example is another highly effective way to establish and sustain a positive influence with your team.

Transactional Leadership is another leadership style that's supported by power and influence theories. This approach assumes that the work only gets done because it is followed by a reward and for that reason only. Therefore it focuses on designing tasks and reward structures. While it may not be the most appealing leadership strategy in terms of building relationships and developing a long-term motivating work environment, it does work, and it's used in most organizations on a daily basis to get things done.

With so many theories and approaches to leadership, there's an underlying message here and that is leaders need to have a variety of factors working in their favor. Effective leadership is not based on a simple set of attributes or behaviors but as an effective leader you need to have a wide range of abilities to help you reach the audience that you are trying to lead.

Transformational Leadership is the one leadership style that is usually appropriate in most corporate situations. A leader using this style:

- Has integrity.
- Sets clear goals.
- Clearly communicates a vision.
- Sets a good example.
- Expects the best from the team.
- Encourages.
- Supports.
- Recognizes good work and people.

- Provides stimulating work
- Helps people see beyond their self interest and focus more on team interests and needs.
- Inspires

Transformational leaders are very good at motivating, and are normally well trusted. When your team trusts you, and is inspired by the way you lead, you can normally achieve great things!

The transformational leadership style is the most dominant of the leadership styles taught today, although other styles are recommended as the situation demands.

Transformational leadership suits many circumstances in business and we should remember that there are always situations where it may not be the best style to use. The leadership theories and styles that we've discussed up until this point are based on research. However, many more terms can be used to describe the different approaches to leadership, even if they don't fit within a particular theoretical system.

Autocratic Leadership

Autocratic leadership is an extreme form of transactional leadership, where leaders have absolute power over their workers or team. There is very little opportunity for staff or team members to make suggestions, even if it would be in the best interest of the team or organization.

This type of leadership usually leads to high levels of absenteeism and staff turnover. For some routine and unskilled jobs, the style can remain effective because the advantages of control may outweigh the disadvantages.

Bureaucratic Leadership

Bureaucratic leaders are always working "by the book." They follow rules rigorously, and ensure that their staff follows procedures as well. This style is appropriate when working in dangerous or unsafe situations that may involve risks (such as working with machinery, with toxic substances, or at dangerous heights) or where large sums of money are involved (such as handling cash).

Charismatic Leadership

Charismatic leaders are similar to transformational leaders in that they inspire enthusiasm in their teams and lots of energy. However, charismatic leaders can tend to believe more in themselves than in their teams, and this could cause the entire organization to collapse if the leader leaves. Success is directly tied to the presence of the charismatic leader. As such, charismatic leadership carries a much greater responsibility, and it needs a long- term commitment from the leader.

Democratic Leadership

Democratic leaders make the final decision but they invite other team members to contribute to the decision-making process. Not only does this increase job satisfaction but it also helps to develop people's skills. Team members feel more in control of their own destiny and career, so they're inclined to work harder for more than just a financial reward.

Because participation takes time, this approach can take more time, but often the end result is better. The approach can be most suitable when working as a team is essential, and when quality is more important than speed to market or productivity.

Laissez-Faire Leadership

This phrase is French for "leave it be," and describes a leader who leaves their team members to work on their own. This technique can be effective if the leader takes the time to monitor what is being achieved and regularly communicates with the team. This style of leadership is most effective when team members are very experienced, skilled or self- starters.

People-Oriented Leadership

With people-oriented leadership, a leader is totally focused on the organizing, supporting, and developing of the teams. It's a participative style, and tends to focus more on good teamwork and creative collaboration.

Servant Leadership

In the 1970's Robert Greenleaf coined the term servant leadership to describe a leader that is often not necessarily recognized as a leader. When someone, at any level in an organization, leads simply by meeting the needs of the team, he or she is described as a "servant leader."

Servant leadership is a form of democratic leadership, because the whole team can become involved in the decision making process.

Many supporters of the servant leadership model suggest that it's an important way to move ahead in a world where values are becoming increasingly important, and where servant leaders achieve power on the basis of their values and ideals. Most political candidates campaign on the servant leadership model. They try to gain your vote by connecting their values and ideals to your belief system. Others believe that in competitive leadership situations, people who practice servant leadership can find themselves left behind by leaders using other leadership styles.

Task-Oriented Leadership

Task-oriented leaders are very good at focusing only on getting the job done. In a very autocratic way they define the work and the roles required, they put structures in place, plan, organize, and monitor. However, because task-oriented leaders don't tend to think much about the well-being of their teams, this approach can suffer many of the flaws of autocratic leadership, with difficulties in motivating and retaining staff. This style could result in a costly style of management if you have to constantly recruit and replace staff due to a high turnover rate.

Transactional Leadership

A leadership style that starts with the idea that team members will agree to obey their leader totally when they accept the job. The "transaction" is usually the organization compensating the team members in return for their loyalty and compliance. The leader has a right to "punish" team members if their work doesn't meet the pre-determined standard.

Team members can do very little to improve their job satisfaction under a transactional leader. In some cases the leader may give team members some control of their income/rewards by using incentives that encourage even higher standards or greater productivity. Alternatively, a transactional leader could practice "management by exception" – rather than rewarding better work, the leader could take corrective action if the required standards are not met.

Transactional leadership is really a type of management, not a true leadership style, because it is mostly focused on short-term tasks and has serious limitations for knowledge-based or creative work.

Transformational Leadership

One of the most popular leadership styles, transformational leaders are true leaders who inspire their teams with a shared vision of the future.

Transformational leaders have an innate ability to pass their level of commitment and enthusiasm on to the team, but they also need support by "other people." That's why, in many organizations, both transactional and transformational leadership is needed. The transactional leader (or manager) ensures that routine work is done, while the transformational leader provides the leadership needed for value added tasks.

While the transformational leadership approach is often highly effective, there's no one "right" way to lead or manage people that fits every situation. In order to determine the most effective approach for yourself, you should consider the following:

- The various skill levels and experience of your team members.

- The type of work involved (routine, new, innovative).

- The organizational environment (stable or radically changing, conservative or adventurous).

- Your own preferred or natural management style.

Good leaders will often switch instinctively between leadership styles, depending on the people they lead and the work that needs to be accomplished. The likelihood of success increases dramatically when there is a high level of trust within the organization and the leader has the ability to balance the needs of the organization against the needs of the team.

How will you be rated?

Now in the world of management most people don't seem to realize that in some organizations managers have managers both above and below them. This is where we get the term middle manager. It depends on where you are in the management food chain as to how you are rated.

Most managers who have subordinate managers that they supervise, rate their subordinate manager on two or three main issues. How well they deliver, how well you protect them and are they profitable or within budget?

What you as a subordinate or entry level manager need to understand is that your organization is your supervisors' organization. Your performance affects the overall performance of your superiors. If you fail they either fail or look bad in the eyes of their management. If you do great things then they are seen as an effective leader who gets things done.

Here's a bit of career advice. If you are a good employee, then your boss probably likes you. If you are a great employee then your boss is probably going to want to take you with them to their next job assignment which could mean more money in your future as you may get promoted to continue to protect them and make them look good.

Expectations

Do your employees know what you expect? Are they being mentally challenged everyday? If your employees are not being challenged with meaningful work that keeps them busy trying to improve on the product or service at hand they will (by human nature) find other things to challenge or entertain them like the internet or long personal phone calls at their desk. Once this behavior begins to happen you will lose productivity within your workforce and that will eventually start to cost you money as you unknowingly hire people to help finish the work that the bored staff is not completing. If the work is too challenging for them then those that are dead weight will move on, those that are go getters will move up.

CHAPTER NOTES

How to Lead a Meeting

" PRODUCTIVITY IS NEVER AN ACCIDENT. IT IS ALWAYS THE RESULT OF A COMMITMENT TO EXCELLENCE, INTELLIGENT PLANNING, AND FOCUSED EFFORT." – PAUL J MEYER

One of the most common complaints among many organizations is meetings. There are just too many meetings, meetings that last too long, meetings that accomplish nothing, meetings to plan other meetings and no actions are ever taken after the meeting is held are amongst the biggest criticisms we've heard.

In today's team-oriented structure, it's almost impossible to avoid having meetings. Many organizations allow decisions to be made by the group, and important information is best-shared face-to-face. Meetings can help to reduce if not alleviate misunderstandings that can easily arise if information is not communicated clearly.

Many meetings are often necessary and important, but when they are poorly run, they have very little productive value and can cause resentment or tension among those who have to attend.

If all your meetings are poorly run it can leave participants unwilling to attend, providing you with lame excuses or delegating a staffer to attend because they just realized they had another meeting scheduled at the same time. How many times have you left a meeting thinking, "I could have been doing so many other things while I wasted time sitting through this meeting!" Do people ever have that impression after your meetings? Running a meeting properly can help make or break your leadership effectiveness. If you keep a few simple guidelines in mind you can vastly improve the meetings you are involved in.

Regardless of whether your meetings are large or small, you should still try to be somewhat organized.

Consider the following "rules" to improve your meetings.

- Be very clear and concise about the reason for having the meeting. Determine if there are any decisions that must be made?

- Is there any information that must be dispensed or pre-read before the meeting?

- Are there particular projects that you expect updated reports on?

- If after asking yourself these kinds of questions, you determine that you have no clear need to have a meeting, cancel it

63

sooner than later. Your staff will appreciate it more than you know.

- Be sure you prepare an agenda. This is one of the most important things you can do to have more effective meetings. Send out your agenda to the attendees as far in advance as possible so they will have adequate time to come prepared to report on anything they may be responsible for knowing.

- Offering team members the opportunity to suggest agenda items will help you to gain buy-in from them for actually having the meeting.

- Prioritize your agenda and deal with the most critical items first.

- Stick to your meeting times. Begin no more than two minutes after your suggested start time. If you also set an ending time, this will encourage you to make the most of your limited time. End the meeting when you say you will end, so you are respectful of people's time. If you didn't get everything covered, carry these items over to the next meeting and place them first on the new agenda.

- Be sure to keep control of the meeting and don't let people ramble on and on while speaking. If participants get off track, remind them assertively and politely to get back to the issue at hand so you can end the meeting on time.

- Just as you work to prevent rambling you must also not let people engage in side battles. If it becomes clear that two participants are at odds, assign them to discuss their differences privately offline and move on to the next item.

- Follow-up is critical to managing successful meetings. Other than having an agenda, the next most important thing you can do is to have a scribe make notes of all decisions made and tasks assigned. Distribute the notes to attendees and anyone else who should know what has transpired during the meeting.

Remember

- Know what you intend to accomplish, and use an agenda.

- Keep the meeting as short and focused as possible.

- Distribute a summary of decisions made and actions assigned.

- Keep people moving by following up with them to be sure they are completing action items by the assigned due date(s).

CHAPTER NOTES

Building Teamwork

" TALENT WINS GAMES, BUT TEAMWORK AND INTELLIGENCE WINS CHAMPIONSHIPS." – MICHAEL JORDAN

Teamwork can be as easy or complicated as we make it. The following is an example of a small and growing company that had a difficult time transitioning with their rapid growth. The company in this scenario did excellent work and was committed to the mission of serving their customers. Over a period of about 20 years they had grown at a slow and steady pace through word of mouth referrals because of their exceptional customer service. In the last two years, they have grown at a record pace, but with that growth came a few new problems.

The owner of what started out as a very small company continued to try and be everything to all people and be involved in everyday decisions of what was now a much larger, faster moving company. The owner had become stretched thin and was noticeably exhausted. The employees were getting frustrated, decisions were being made at a snails pace, conflict was a daily occurrence, and morale was poor. Turf wars were a common occurrence, and a lack of teamwork was a real issue as well.

As problems continue to mount the issues have started affecting customer service levels. Despite growth in product demand, customer and employee retention was becoming a huge problem.

Does any of this sound familiar to your organization? How well does your organization function? Is your company having turnover problems? Any problems you observe in these areas may be occurring for a variety of reasons, but whatever the reasons don't feel alone because these types of problems are more commonplace than you would expect.

CHAPTER NOTES

Hiring the Right People for the Job

" I HIRE PEOPLE BRIGHTER THAN ME AND THEN I GET OUT OF THEIR WAY" — LEE IACOCCA

Here is an unfortunate fact, the job market is not just tightening up again, it is literally air tight. Many employment experts have predicted that an increasing number of jobs will go unfilled in the next eight or ten years as many baby boomers retire in droves and the economy remains in flux (as of 2011).

Now this doesn't mean that you have to settle for anything that you can get in an employee. It's more critical than ever that you hire the very best employees you can find. I recommend that you be very selective, even if it takes longer to do so.

Some supervisors, managers, or team leaders may not have the full decision-making authority when it comes to filling a job vacancy, but most managers do have some level of input into the decision. Everyone wants to hire the best possible candidate for the job and you can drastically improve your odds in doing so with a better use of two critical selection tools: reference-checks and interviews.

Checking References

Checking references is a **must.** Let me say that again. Checking references is a **must**. The best predictor of how someone will perform on your job site is how well he or she has performed related jobs in the past. As true as this fact may be, even for managers who have experienced not checking a candidate's references, only to pay for it later, believe it or not, many managers still do not take the time to properly check a candidate's references. Trust me, it is well worth the trouble to do so. During your reference checks you will find that some organizations will give very little information for fear of being sued.

If the old company seems reluctant to share information, work to push them politely for more information. Is there someone else you can talk to? At the very least press them to answer this question: Is this person eligible for rehire? If the answer is yes, this is a pretty good indicator that the applicant was at least acceptable as an employee.

Another approach you might also consider taking is getting the applicant to sign a form (separate from the application) that allows you to contact their previous employer. Get the fax number of that employer and fax your signed permission form to them to document the applicant's willingness to allow an open exchange of information. If an applicant declines to sign such a form, this could be a critical indicator that something may not be as it should.

Good Interviews

As much as I feel it is important to check a candidate's references, having the opportunity to interview them, especially in person can dramatically improve your chances of picking a good quality candidate. If you truly want an objective view of a candidate's potential to succeed in your organization then you should schedule them to have multiple interviews with key people in your organization. Conduct each interview separately or with a group together in the form of a panel interview. Getting the opinions of several others, including one or more of your workers, will give a wider perspective. One person will notice things some of the others won't. I would highly recommend that you do not hire someone that one or more of your panel members have grave doubts about.

Do second interviews with your top candidates—or keep looking.

Even Better Interviews

If the best predictor of future job performance is past job performance, then you can use this to your advantage for candidate interviews. Rather than having a generic set of interview questions like "Tell me about yourself or Tell me about your last job," you can construct several behavioral interview questions that give you excellent clues about your applicant. If you do write such questions, you will also impress your boss and your human resources manager.

In order to develop your behavioral questions, think of two or three qualities that you would like to see in an employee, then write the questions that can probe whether or not your candidate has those qualities. For example, if teamwork is an important qualily that you want to see, you might use interview questions similar to these:

We do a lot of collaborative projects, so teamwork is very important to accomplishing our work. Can you give me an example of a time you worked closely with a group of people. How did you work with them and what did you accomplish?

Tell me about a time you had communication difficulties with a co-worker and how did you handle it?

Another example might be that safety is an important consideration:

Describe a situation on a previous job where you had a concern about safety and what did you do about it?

You can use these ideas to probe for examples of any particular qualities or characteristics that are important to you for your job opportunities.

Be sure to pay attention not only to what they say but their body language and any emotion in their voice. The answers to your interview questions will provide good clues about how each candidate would fit in with your organization, thus improving your chances of selecting the right person for the job.

Retaining Valued Employees

If we believe the information coming out of various human relations and employment studies, employers are facing a period of time where there will be far less qualified employees to select from when replacing a retiring or turnover workforce. There are several factors that contribute to this situation:

- There are fewer 18-21 year olds entering the workforce.

- Many baby boomers (50-something and 60-something workers) will be retiring or looking to reduce their work hours.

- This generation of workers has a drastically different attitude and work ethic than the baby boomers and generation X workforce to which we have become accustomed.

Whether you terminate an employee or they voluntarily leave your organization, employee turnover is an expensive event. Most financial estimates project that the cost of replacing an employee is about 50% of his or her annual salary.

Therefore if you lose three people who earn $50,000 a year, your cost to replace that staff may cost your bottom line upwards of $75,000. This can be a staggering figure if your profits are low or the previous hires were not very productive towards increasing your income or business revenue.

We all know that most employees WANT to do a good job at work. It may not always appear that way but rarely does an employee want to sabotage or destroy their employers

83

business on purpose. They just may not assume that their behavior is having that great of an effect on the company's success.

There have been many times when I have had an employee say "my job isn't that important," but in reality it is, they just don't understand their role in the success of others who may get all the accolades or have the fancy titles with the big paychecks.

When the supply of qualified workers becomes a commodity, it is very important to retain your current workforce by any means necessary. Everyone wants to live the best life that they can and studies show that 30-60% of the workforce is actively looking for a new job at any given time; even if they are not actively looking, they may have the attitude of being "open" to a better situation. If they hear of a good opportunity or they get a call from a headhunter, what's to prevent them from leaving you for a higher salary, better work hours or a shorter commute to the office?

The only thing that can prevent them from leaving your organization is YOU. Here's how you do it: Show your appreciation and gain their loyalty. Employees who feel unappreciated are far more likely to quit, are less likely to be highly motivated while on the job, and are more likely to be absent or tardy. Those that have a sense of loyalty to you are less likely to leave you in a lurch and are more willing to support your efforts for a successful workforce.

Tips to retaining your workforce:

- Make sure your people have adequate communications from management and senior leadership. If the way that they perform their jobs will change, have they gotten clear instruction on how they will need to comply with their new job tasks? It is up to you to make sure they know how their jobs will change and that they are as comfortable with the new process as possible before it is implemented. They will respect you and your leadership style much more as a result. When possible, provide instructions both verbally and in written form (for reference).

- Be sure your employees know your expectations for deadline dates, finished product quality, or performance numbers—especially if any of these items/expectations have recently changed.
- Help them to understand "why" we are doing it "this way," now instead of the

"old way." When you explain why, your employees feel more engaged in the process because they now know the whole story. Knowing "why" helps them to feel more appreciated and a more significant part of the team.

• Look for opportunities to praise your employees and show gratitude. Recognize them for the good they do, even if what the employee did is part of their usual job responsibilities.

• Regularly, thank them for work they performed well especially if it was team-oriented. Be as immediate and focused as possible when you thank or praise an employee; otherwise, it may sound phony or manipulative. "You're great," is less effective than saying, "Thanks for dropping everything yesterday to get the Bateman proposal revised."

• You should routinely ask your employees what they need in order to do their jobs better, what would help them? But if you have little intention of following through, don't even ask!

Remember that your most important role as a manager, supervisor, or team leader is to help your employees succeed.

If you ignore or minimize employee concerns and they start to assume that you do not care about them they will systematically start to care less about you, the company and your mission. If they get that perception you are likely to see an increased rate of turnover as people begin to look for a better opportunity. If turnover is already high in your organization, take an honest look at your management – staff relationship and access what the perceptions are and what you need to do to change them. Remember an undervalued employee will give you exactly what they are feeling, LESS VALUE for your money. Set a personal goal for yourself to show more appreciation to all your employees on a regular basis. You will be surprised how quickly things will turn around for you.

CHAPTER NOTES

Counseling Employees with Performance Problems

" HARSH COUNSELS HAVE NO EFFECT; THEY ARE LIKE HAMMERS, WHICH ARE ALWAYS REPULSED BY THE ANVIL" — CLAUDE ADRIEN HELVETIUS

The act of counseling an employee who has not performed satisfactorily during some rating period throughout the year is second only to performing your own root canal. The importance of addressing problems with employees in the very early stages cannot be stressed enough. The very moment an issue surfaces you should address it with a positive confrontation.

If your organization has an employee relations manager it is highly recommended to meet with them prior to your meeting with the employee.

The employee relations manager will be able to advise you on the correct approach, documentation, and rights both you and the employee are afforded during the process. Most managers and supervisors are regularly presented with the need to address a performance issue.

Unfortunately, too many leaders don't do it, which is why you are probably having problems with the same employee now.

How do you deal with undertaking such an unpleasant issue when you have so many other things to take care of and this is your least favorite type of conversation to boot? What words and approach will be effective in changing the employee's performance or behavior, while minimizing the risk of losing them?

Turnover is expensive, and if the employee has any potential, it's definitely worth the effort to try to save him or her. If you tend to put this kind of a discussion off, give yourself an incentive by remembering that it's definitely costing you money. One poor performer can decrease productivity and lower office morale for your entire team.

If you're having difficulty regarding how to have these conversations and continuously put them off you are only digging your grave deeper. Remember you are the manager and it is your responsibility to maintain a highly productive work unit or your supervisor may need to find someone else who can.

Planning and Executing the Counseling (Coaching) Session

The best approach to take is to speak to the employee in person if at all possible (or by telephone if they are located at a distance) and schedule an appointment that is mutually convenient. By scheduling a formal meeting with them, they will not be caught off guard and it lends a sense of seriousness to the event for the employee. Let them know what you want to talk about regarding their performance. Be as calm and non-threatening as you can when you inform them of this desired meeting, but say it directly and in a business-like tone. Be sure to schedule adequate enough time for this meeting to take place. It's not just you, the manager or supervisor, who will need time to talk; you will be trying to create a dialogue in this session, so be sure to allow time for that to happen.

Prior to your meeting, do your homework. Be sure you can describe clearly what the issue is: Is it a performance problem? A conduct problem? Jot down specific instances or evidence that support your concern. Plan what you will say to your employee before your meeting. It's especially helpful to write it down and commit your first few sentences to memory. This will help you feel more confident. Writing it down will help you clearly say what you mean and, at the same time, keep your anger in check.

Schedule a time when you can speak to the person privately at a place where you will not be overheard—a conference room, your office or the employee's office. Don't use a cubicle where you can—and probably will—be overheard.

It's helpful to begin the coaching/counseling session with an opening statement such as: John "I have a problem that I need your help in solving." Maintain that kind of attitude and intention! Asking for someone's help is less threatening to them than beginning with an accusation. After your opening statement, continue to describe the details of the issue and the evidence you compiled during your homework. Do not make accusations or evaluations at this point just stick with the facts.

Once you have taken a few minutes to describe your concerns, invite the employee'scomments or perceptions. A statement something like, "Tell me what's going on with you?" helps draw the employee into a dialogue. At this point, it's important that you stop talking and listen openly.

Don't try to formulate your next response while they are talking. Do they have some points, some explanation, or some information you were unaware of? Acknowledge any points they may have. If what they offer is excuses, you need to stick to your guns. Don't be trapped into solving the employee's problem or accepting their excuses. Challenge their excuses and help them problem-solve by asking something like: "So what actions can you take to be sure you do not oversleep again?"

Be as kind as possible, but once you have listened to their side of the story be sure that you clearly state what your expectations are for adequate performance in their current job. If you have done a good job describing their behavior in your opening comments and now have described what good performance should look like, point out the gap between their performance and what is expected. Ask them for ideas on what they need to help them move from their level of performance to the acceptable level. Do they need help from you? Additional training? Jointly develop a plan of action and agree what the employee will do and by what date these actions will be completed. The plan of action will be different depending on whether the problem is one of deficient performance or an issue of conduct.

Some managers and supervisors do fairly well up to this point. In order to be successful in dealing with performance problems, however, it is crucial that you both document your session and follow-up on your agreement.

To document, write down the date and time of the meeting, the employee's name, the issue discussed, and the plan of action you both agreed to; sign and date your documentation. It's important to keep a record of this discussion (Find out where in your organization this should be kept). In your own files? In the Human Resources Office? Keep the documentation factual, with no evaluative comments. It's also a good idea to send a copy to the employee to remind the employee of the changes she or he agreed to make to address this issue.

Before concluding your first counseling or coaching session, establish another appointment with your employee to revisit the issue(s). Agree to schedule a follow-up meeting to discuss the progress of any proposed action plan that would be used to correct the unwanted behavior. Whether it is 2 days, 3 weeks or 30 days, do not fail to schedule this follow- up meeting. If you do, you will fall victim to letting your employee think that if you don't call them in to speak with them again, that everything must be ok. You as their manager must be satisfied with the improvements they've made. Don't let them have to assume the situation has improved. If the situation has improved let them know that too, it shows that you really care about their progression. If nothing has changed at the time of the follow-up meeting, your employee should be told that you may need to initiate the additional steps of progressive discipline which could result in the termination of their employment if the issue does not begin to improve.

If you think having the initial conversation is tough then prepare yourself to deal with an employee that has made little to no progress by the time a follow- up meeting occurs.

If he or she is making positive changes which you can identify, it may be a good idea to set a second follow-up meeting by which time clear, consistent, and specific changes should have been made that meet specific performance standards, or progressive discipline will be initiated. The number of counseling sessions you have with your underperforming employee will depend largely on your company's culture and policies. In most instances, having one session before formal disciplinary action takes place is a good idea. More than two such sessions, however, may be ineffective; if the employee gets the impression that management is all talk and no action they will not put any effort into the need to improve. If an employee cannot or will not improve, you are better served by terminating their employment and using the techniques listed in the previous chapter to interview and hire someone else who can better serve your needs.

If you take proactive steps to deal with your underperforming employees as described above, you are likely to be able to help them more often than not, meet management's expectations and become a better employee.

CHAPTER NOTES

Strategies to Motivate and Lead

" LEADERS MUST BE CLOSE ENOUGH TO RELATE TO OTHERS, BUT FAR ENOUGH AHEAD TO MOTIVATE THEM." — JOHN MAXWELL

The following are some simple, inexpensive ideas you can use to demonstrate a sense of strong leadership within your organization. You can use these ideas as written or use them to help you create better or more relevant ideas for your own management situation.

These inspirations will help you to increase your employee's motivation level and develop a culture of commitment among your staff. The more enjoyable a place is to work the less people are concerned about the size of their paycheck. This is not to say that they don't want to earn a good living but they are less likely to leave your organization that is known as a great place to work for a few more dollars than you are willing to pay them. If they leave to go to the competition then the competition will have to pay dearly to get them to risk crossing over to the other side.

- Keep a list of prizes, from small to large, everything from company logo items, tickets to special events, gift cards, and contributions to their favorite charity. Let your employees choose a prize, when they are recognized by a peer or manager for an organizational contribution. The value of the reward should be comparable to the value of the contribution.

- Create a Hero Jar and encourage employees to nominate each other for outstanding achievements on the job. The nomination forms should allow space to describe what the achievement was and should include the name of the person nominating the achievement. The winning nominations should be read each month at an all employees or group staff meeting which all relevant employees or team members attend. The winner gets a gift card or similar prize.

- What does your company provide or produce that could be given out to employees for free? For example, a restaurant could give out a monthly dinner for two for a year or a car lot can give a free loaner car for the month, maybe it is as simple as a special parking space right in front of the building at work, you would be surprised how little a gift prize will cost you to keep your employees happy and motivated.

- Give high-performing employees a progressive training opportunity as a special assistant to one of the company executives, including attending executive team meetings. They learn a great deal more about how the company really works and it increases their commitment to the organization, not to mention the career opportunities that it may hold from the experience and new relationships that they can gain.

- Offer employees an increase in pay or a small bonus when they take on additional responsibilities that are challenging; for example, serving on a critical work team or special task-force or project development team.

- If you have a sales force (or distributors) and you rely on their knowledge and expertise for your product sales, you can create a knowledge contest. Your reps could call a phone number to answer quiz questions or complete an online test. Those who obtain a certain score would receive a prize. All those who pass receive an internal certification and their names are entered into a drawing for a nice prize.

- Create a suggestion box. If the employee's suggestion is the winner for the month they receive 4 to 8 hours of administrative or personal leave. This is an excellent way to solicit ideas that can help your company grow and keep your workforce motivated at the same time.

- Turn the general mood from negative to positive by creating a "Good Things" Wall. Put up a large piece of butcher paper and attach a marker in a break room or someplace else that employees frequently access. Write down anything that has gone well in the organization, from small things to large ones, and encourage others to record the successes they see. Encourage participation by assigning someone to go to each employee weekly to find out from them, "what was the best thing that happened to you at work this week?"

- Some workplaces have known downtimes, you could rent a DVD for your entire team or for those employees recognized for outstanding performance by their managers or peers to view as a perk for a job well done.

- Have your boss or an executive attend the meetings in which you thank or recognize employees or team members for outstanding performance.

- You could also recognize the work of your entire team by having a catered lunch brought in to celebrate the completion of a major milestone.

- Award your employees a bonus for every customer compliment.

CHAPTER NOTES

Avoiding the Micromanagement Trap

" AND I'M THE KIND OF MANAGER THAT DOESN'T BELIEVE THAT YOU MICRO-MANAGE PROFESSIONALS. THEY SHOULD UNDERSTAND THEIR RESPONSIBILITY AND CARRY OUT THOSE RESPONSIBLY." — *ALPHONSO JACKSON*

Helping Team Members Excel on Their Own

There is no faster way to the management Hall of Shame than if you become known as a consistent micromanager.

If you assign an important task to one of your best employees, and give them clear instructions on what you would like the final outcome to be, do you constantly look over their shoulder and tell them how to perform the tasks or do you let them do their work and simply touch base with them at pre- defined points along the way?

If you are constantly dropping hints at how to perform the next task, you are probably a closet micromanager. You have got to work hard to let go and simply hold your employees accountable for the expectations that you have set for them.

Micromanagers are people that tend to take every little detail to the extreme, either because they're obsessed with having total control or because they feel the need to push everyone in order to be a success on all their projects.

Many times micromanagers end up disempowering their employees more than they help them. Working for a micromanager can result in employees or colleagues' losing confidence in themselves or their abilities, their professional growth and development being stiffled, or it can begin to create confusion, which may affect their performance and frustrate them to the point where they quit or start to look for other opportunities.

Remember turnover can cost you up to 50% of their salary to replace them.

If you're not sure you are a micromanager here are a few signs that might help you recognize this potentially destructive behavior and draw the line between being a involved manager or an over-involved supervisor who's driving his team mad?

Signs of micromanagement

- You have a problem delegating;
- You immerse yourself in overseeing the projects of others;
- Your start by correcting the smallest of details instead of looking at the big picture;
- You take back delegated work before it is finished if you find a mistake in it; and
- You discourage others from making simple decisions.

What's wrong with micromanaging? You are getting things done on time and within budget so why not keep using the micromanagement style to maintain your performance record?

Micromanagers often affirm the value of their management style with a simple test:

They will give an employee an assignment and then disengage until the deadline. Will the employee excel when given free rein to work on the project alone?

If the employee has exceptional confidence in his or her abilities then they more than likely will be able to handle everything that comes with competing priorities and completing the work. Under a micromanagement style, however, most workers become timid and tentative - possibly even paralyzed. "No matter what I do," such a worker might think to themselves, "It won't be good enough." When this mindset sinks in, one of two things may happen: Either they will ask the manager for additional guidance before the deadline or they will forge ahead, but come up with an inadequate result.

In either case, the micromanager will interpret the result of his experiment as proof that, without his constant intervention, his people will flounder or fail.

An effective manager creates an environment for others to succeed. Micromanagers, whether consciously or not, prevent employees from making and taking responsibility for their own actions. It's the process of making decisions, and

119

living with the consequences that cause people to grow and improve professionally.

If you want to be a great manager, empower your employees and give them opportunities to excel. Bad managers have a tendency to unempower their employees by restricting those growth opportunities. A disempowered employee is an ineffective one. If you don't think you have a lot of time on your hands now, try managing employees who feel disempowered, they require a lot more time and energy than employees that have been empowered.

It's all that extra time and energy that throws off your day as a manager, making you ineffective. If you multiply that time and energy across a whole team of timid workers, it will amount to a serious drain of energy on your time. It's extremely difficult, if not impossible, to keep up with your team and the other "big" tasks of managing people when you are sweating the small details of the next sales presentation.

CHAPTER NOTES

Mentoring the Glue that Holds it All Together

MENTORING IS A BRAIN TO PICK. AN EAR TO LISTEN. AND A PUSH IN THE RIGHT DIRECTION." — JOHN CROSBY

The building of a high performing team is a key part of being recognized as an effective leader.

Becoming a mentor will allow you to help employees both within and outside of your team to learn, grow, and become more effective in their jobs. This is why mentoring is such an important leadership skill.

What is Mentoring? Mentoring is a relationship between two people with the goal of developing them both professionally and personally. The "mentor" is usually an experienced individual who shares their knowledge, experience and advice with a less experienced person, or "mentee."

A mentor becomes a trusted adviser and role model. A mentor is the person who has typically "been there" and "done that." The mentor supports and encourages their mentee by offering advice, both general and specific. Your goal should be to help your mentees improve their skills and hopefully, advance their careers.

Benefits of Mentoring?

Mentoring can be extremely rewarding for you, both personally and professionally. Successful mentoring can also help you to build a stronger and more successful team, while also improving your leadership and communication skills, learning new perspectives and ways of thinking, while also gaining a strong sense of personal satisfaction.

For mentees, the benefits of mentoring can be immense. They get focused coaching and training from a skilled, knowledgeable and experienced individual, they also get assistance and advice in how to navigate the various management situations that will arise in the workplace. This type of advise can help them work more effectively, and overcome obstacles that would otherwise slow or stall their careers.

Even if the benefits of mentoring sound like a great idea, you have to decide whether this sort of time- consuming, relationship is right for you and for the person you're thinking of mentoring. If the mentoring relationship has arisen informally and spontaneously, then the chances are that things are fine.   However, if you're taking a more formal approach to mentoring, it's worth exploring your reasons for mentoring and asking yourself whether you want to take this type of commitment further. To do so, ask yourself these questions:

- Is mentoring the best way of developing the knowledge, skills and abilities that the potential mentee needs? Or would other approaches be quicker or more effective?

- How will mentoring contribute toward your own career goals, and to the goals of your team and your organization?

- Is mentoring a particular individual a good use of your time and are you comfortable that you'll be able to devote time to him or her on a regular basis?

- Do you have the knowledge, skills and experience that the mentee is likely to find helpful?

- How much personal satisfaction are you likely to get from the relationship? Does this justify your involvement and do you like the individual enough to want to invest time in mentoring him or her on a regular basis?

- In what areas are you willing to help? Are there any areas that you don't want to go near?

What You Should Consider

Although you may want to jump right in with both feet, make sure that you also think about these practical considerations:

- Formality of approach – Do you want to take a relaxed, ad hoc approach to mentoring, or do you want to approach sessions in a more structured, formal way?

- Frequency of contact – How much time can you commit to this relationship?

- Can you meet (however you do that) weekly? Biweekly? Once a month?

- How long can you spend in each meeting? Half an hour? An hour? More?

- Do you want to be available between "formal" sessions?

- Method of contact – Would you prefer face-to-face meetings, phone calls, or emails? If you are to use the phone call method, who places the call?

- Duration of partnership – Do you want to limit the length of the mentoring partnership? Do you want to set regular intervals to review whether you're both happy with the relationship, or do you just want to informally review progress on an ongoing basis?

- Confidentiality – How will you approach confidential business information? Think of ways to speak about general concepts and situations while maintaining confidentiality.

Where to Draw the Line

When developing a mentoring relationship, make sure you have clear boundaries of what you can and cannot do for the mentee.

Answer the above questions to help yourself define the boundaries for the relationship. Then, when you're meeting, you'll better understand your own mindset – what areas you're interested in covering, and what you will and will not do.

Take the lead on where you'll allow the mentoring relationship to go and what ground you'll cover. As a general guide, focus on your expertise and experience. If anything is beyond your skills and abilities, refer the mentee to another expert.

For example, if a discussion about human resources issues raises a concern about employment law, consider sending your mentee to an internal expert or attorney. If conversations about work problems lead into personal or family problems, the mentee may need more focused professional help from a psychologist or therapist.

As a mentor, you can become the mentee's confidante and adviser. You may be called upon to be a "sounding board" for all sorts of issues and concerns. So know in advance how you're going to deal with difficult situations.

Key Points

- By mentoring effectively, you can do a lot to improve the performance of key individuals within your team, thereby helping yourself reach team and organizational goals.

- Mentoring can also give you a great overall sense of personal satisfaction, knowing that you're helping someone else learn and grow on a professional and personal level.

Before you begin a mentoring partnership, it's useful to think about your reasons for becoming a mentor and the practical considerations and logistics of such a relationship. If you decide that mentoring is right for you, the time and effort that you put into it can reap great rewards that far exceed your expectations.

CHAPTER NOTES

Leadership is it an Art or Science

" LIFE IMITATES ART FAR MORE THAN ART IMITATES LIFE." –
OSCAR WILDE

Regardless of whether you are or were a leader in high school, college, your community or on your job, leadership is and always will be more of an art than it is a science.

If you have not realized it yet, every leadership situation will require several different skillsets based on the personnel, conditions and situations being addressed.

There is no magic combination of skills that will make you a textbook leader, destined to achieve greatness, but there is one trait that I believe all leaders must have and that is courage. A true leader must have the courage to forge ahead and address issues or go places that others have refused to go. This quality is what separates leaders from managers.

Remaining true to yourself and your core beliefs may sometimes seem hard when the world says otherwise, but no one ever said leading was going to be as easy as some of us make it look. You see anyone can manage a situation through appointed power, because people generally will do as you say, but only a true leader can maximize the resources at their disposal to achieve extraordinary results with ordinary people.

Remember, regardless of what leadership style you choose, you can only lead using a style that fits you and your personality. If you take care of the people the people will always take care of you.

You can lead a horse to water but you can't make them drink. You can stand in the front of the room, but that does not mean everyone will follow you. For those that do follow you, use what you have learned from this book to make that journey a successful one.

By now I hope I have given you some real insight into how successful leaders achieve their greatness. What you do with your newly found knowledge is up to you. Now go out there and LEAD!

CHAPTER NOTES

ABOUT THE INTERNATIONAL
LEADERSHIP CORPORATION

An innovator in corporate training and organizational performance the International Leadership Corporation helps teams and organizations achieve the results they care about the most.

With training programs based on your specific organizational business needs we provide your team with custom training services to help you solve your organization's most pressing issues.

Each course or presentation is designed to help you leverage your staff's skills, strengths and strategies to create a five star organization.

www.leadershipcorporation.com

INDEX

Lead to Succeed and You Won't Manage to Fail

www.ingramcontent.com/pod-product-compliance
Lightning Source LLC
Chambersburg PA
CBHW032304210326
41520CB00047B/1204